Saved By Grace Through Faith

Charles Matondo

Michael Terence
Publishing

First published in paperback by
Michael Terence Publishing in 2020
www.mtp.agency

ISBN 9781800941014

CONTENTS

ACKNOWLEDGEMENTS

My foremost gratitude is reserved for the almighty God who is the source of my strength, revelation, wisdom and understanding of salvation.

I would like to dedicate this book to my family, beginning with my wife Mrs Matondo who is my first support and motivator and she is always on my side to help me fulfil my dreams. I would also like to acknowledge my children who continue to inspire and encourage me every day. Thank you all for your support in every moment.

There have also been a number of other supporters that have provided a word of encouragement and motivation on my journey of ministry including the members of the Destined to Reign Church (where I am a Pastor) who kept me in their hearts and prayers throughout the process and to them I extend many thanks.

INTRODUCTION

The purpose of this book is to explore the concept of being saved by grace through faith, which is made possible through the work of our Lord Jesus Christ and which has been bestowed upon humankind as an unmerited favour. The favour of God is an irrevocable presence in the life of the believer. In referring to the notion of 'grace', one should not merely consider the word nor its linguistic connotations but rather focus upon the person of Jesus and all that he has accomplished for humankind through his suffering, death, resurrection and his sitting on the throne of glory. The Lord Jesus has made an extraordinary sacrifice for humankind and it is important or individuals to recognise the scale of his achievements in order to live the fullness of the life of God that we have through Christ. The good news of Jesus Christ and knowledge of his sacrifice which bestowed upon humankind the grace of God, a free gift from the Lord provides hope and fortifies individual faith. The good news concerns Jesus Christ is the power of God to free everyone who believes it. We cannot talk about Jesus without exploring what he has fulfilled for humanity as this is the plan of God to save the entire world.

It is God's will that individuals live the life which was made possible through the death and resurrection of His son Jesus Christ. He further desires that individuals live in perfect health and achieve success in all areas of their lives.

God sent His son Jesus to fulfil these wishes on the cross, so that we can experience the abundance of His blessings which extend to all areas of our lives.

God loves us with an immutable and unconditional love and we are very special to Him and carries your picture in His wallet. Awareness of this love promotes a feeling of inner peace and tranquillity which is above anything. God has poured unconditional love out into our hearts as a source of an unmerited favour and humankind is truly living with a blessing that it did not deserve.

This book is divided into six distinctive chapters and a summary conclusion. The first chapter explores definitions of 'grace' and 'faith' and considers how such phenomena function together. The second chapter considers the origins of the concepts of grace, faith and salvation. The third chapter stresses the importance of renewal of the mind for realising the manifestation of God's power in us. The fourth chapter explores the relationship between physical works and grace. The fifth chapter considers the purpose of the Law of Moses and the final chapter concentrating on how the work of Jesus has completed salvation as a done deal that was fulfilled once and for all.

The Holy Spirit will assist you in reading this book to understand that the Salvation of humanity is complete, achieved and we actively live it by faith in the grace of God.

1:

UNDERSTANDING THE CONCEPTS OF GRACE, FAITH AND SALVATION

1.1. What is Grace?

The term 'grace' derives from the Greek 'charis' which is variously interpreted as'the unmerited', 'the undeserved favour', 'good will' and 'goodness'. In the New Covenant this word takes on a meaning of redemption, thereby invoking all that the Lord Jesus Christ has done for us and all that God has made available to humankind which it does not deserve.

Whilst some individuals believe in grace without taking in account of faith, others conversely believe only in faith without taking account of grace. However, the manifestation of the power of God for the delivery of Salvation was made possible through the inter-working of grace and faith. Indeed, neither grace nor faith alone can deliver Salvation and both elements must work together in order to realise the outcomes detailed in the plan of God.

A number of the more frequently cited interpretations of grace include the following:

- *It is what God has done independently of man.*
- *It is the anticipation of God in what man will need.*
- *It is the provision of God for man.*

- *It is a gift of God and it is free because it does not depend on us nor on our performances.*

God has created everything before my existence and all His creation is perfect. The grace of God is unconditional and constant. We do not earn it and we equally do not deserve it. Through the receipt of grace, those who are disqualified are qualified to receive that which they do not deserve. By grace, God has done everything for everybody and we are living on the time of receiving.

It is impossible for an individual to save themselves because the nature of man is incapable of doing good to satisfy God. God created a blueprint for the Salvation of all of humanity and His grace was manifested through the sacrifice of Jesus Christ on Earth which was necessary in order to restore the relationship between God and humankind. The love and the goodness of God have been made freely available to all and His grace represents a special dispensation which was made available from the time on the cross and which cannot be won by the actions of humankind. Therefore, I am the one who supposed to suffer what Jesus had suffered but the love and the goodness of God have offered me the free gifts because all that I have received from God is gift after gift. We do not win the grace but it is the choice and the decision of God for all. Also, grace can be considered as a period (dispensation), as the Bible identifies "the year of grace" that has started from the cross. Grace can be taken as a mentality of receiving from God who is our source.

1.2. What is Faith?

The word 'faith' takes its origin from the Greek 'pistis' which may be interpreted as meaning 'conviction' or 'trust'.

Again, a number of the more often cited interpretations of 'faith' are listed below:

- *It is a positive answer of man in response to all that God has already done by grace.*
- *It is a means of appropriating all that God has already done by grace.*
- *It is what man does to live with all that God has already given to him.*
- *It is the connection of man to God.*
- *It is a bridge between the spiritual reality to the physical reality.*

Faith is the way that gives us access in all that Jesus has already fulfilled, so grace is that God does and faith it is what I use to access the grace.

Hebrew 11:1 – *'Now faith is the substance of things hoped for, the evidence of things not seen.'*(NKJV)

The quotation above identifies faith as the mechanism through which things not seen by the natural eye are evidenced. For example, if a friend were to hide a book behind their back and to enquire as to what they have, you will say nothing because you can't see anything - but in reality, the book exists. Every child of God has received the fullness of the blessings of God and even during times of difficulty and strife, such blessings are still there despite being perceivably absent. This is the nature of the spiritual reality which can be perceived only by faith as what we see physically is not only what is there. Faith is a multidimensional concept and consists of knowing, seeing, accepting and confessing as appropriate. One cannot see something without knowing it cannot accept it without seeing it and cannot confess it without accepting it. Yet how does one 'see' the spiritual realm? This is made possible through the eyes of faith which enable individuals to see all that they possess and the spiritual mirror which promotes reflection in the knowledge of the good news of Jesus Christ. Indeed, collectively faith is the evidence which demonstrates individuals possess already.

The faith of many believers often interpret God's will incorrectly as they do not possess correct and sufficient knowledge and understanding which in turn can lead an individual to live a discordant life. Faith does not mean that God will heal or that they will obtain things but faith believes that God had already healed and blessed – faith is a dynamic concept that function in present continue and indeed an individual must continue to believe until physical manifestation is received.

True knowledge serves as the fuel which enables individuals to explore their faith and maximise their relationship with God. It is for our advantage to have correct information of the life that we have in Christ. A useful analogy is when we buy a new electronic device and do not invest sufficient time in reading the instruction manual. In such circumstances, it is likely that we will not configure the device correctly or use it in accordance with the manufacturers intended function. In this example, the instruction manual (representing the manufacturers' intention) may be compared to the Bible (God's intention) which helps us to understand how to function in our day to day lives and how to live in accordance with all that God has made available for our good.

1.3. The concept of Salvation

For many, the idea of 'Salvation' is a challenging one to understand and is often over-simplified to assertions such as 'our sins have been forgiven' or 'we will not go to hell anymore'. Whilst such comments are partially true, in reality 'Salvation' is a much broader concept than this and incorporates all of the benefits that we have received through the death and the resurrection of Jesus.

The word 'Salvation 'derives from the Greek word 'sozo' which may be interpreted in a myriad of ways including 'forgiveness of sin', 'deliverance', 'eternal life', 'blessing', 'healing', 'justification', 'sanctification', 'victory', 'prosperity', 'peace', 'reconciliation with God', 'protection' and 'authority' amongst others.

Broadly, the word 'Salvation' came from the verb to save and therefore logically when we are saved, we can say that we have achieved Salvation. It is the act of taking someone out of danger and was foretold to Joseph by an angel who told him that 'your wife Mary will bring forth a son and you shall call him Jesus, for he will save his people from their sins…' (Matthew 1:21). Jesus is our saviour who removed us from the danger the sin by restoring the relationship between God and humankind. Man was created in the nature of God and God had lost control of His representative on Earth. Indeed, God had formed the body of man from dust on the ground (the first Adam) and all of humanity was subsequently created in his likeness. When Adam was disobedient to God, it was as if all of humanity disobeyed him also. When Adam was excommunicated from the presence of God, all of humanity was discharged also.

Salvation is a gift from God which, like material human offerings, must be accepted and received. Many have not yet achieved Salvation for the simple reason that they have not yet accepted and received the gift of Salvation that God has given to all of humanity. In the mind and plan of God, everybody has already been saved, however each one of us has the responsibility to accept and to receive the Salvation. But how is one to accomplish this? Simply by believing in the death and the resurrection of Jesus Christ which served to restore the relationship between God and humanity and which made possible the prospect of Salvation. This is a free gift from God available to all and may be contrasted with a gift that is earned through merit i.e. one which requires works to be undertaken prior to receipt.

If someone bought you a gift and asking you to pay a little money back, it means this is not a free gift anymore. When an individual has received Salvation by faith, this means that they have received the full package with everything that is inside. If we believe that our sins have been forgiven, we must also believe that we have been healed from sickness, that we are justified and protected and that we have been blessed with God's grace.

James 5:15 – *'And the prayer of faith will save the sick…'* (NKJV)

Literally, the quotation from the book of James set out above reaffirms that the prayer of faith save the sick and the word "save" has the meaning of "heal". The word save cannot only limited to some benefits because salvation is including all that Jesus has done. In another words, when someone is saved will be granted forgiveness of sin, deliverance from evil, divine health, entering the Kingdom of God as a result of their decision to believe and receive Jesus as the saviour. Similar links between the forgiveness of sins and the healing of illness are recounted in the same verse in Psalm 103:2-3. 1 Peter 2: 24, whereby Peter tells us how Jesus bore our sins in his body and by his stripes we were healed. For many, such truths are difficult to comprehend as they fail to appreciate the magnitude of the sacrifice which Jesus has made for all. Jesus' work impacts upon all areas of our lives including spiritually, mentally and the physical body. Any negative feeling people has not root anymore because the solution to any ailments you may suffer is already within you and whilst the devil may intimidate you, but be conscious that you are already more than conquerors and you have divine health in you.

1.4. Exploring the interaction between Grace and Faith

Many believe that everything depends upon God and that we have nothing to do. According to this perspective, God has already determined who will be saved and who will be lost, thereby suggesting that His favour is destined to only be received by a certain group of people. However, Matthew 25:41 notes that God does not prepare individuals for hell. By virtue of the cross, God forgave the sins of the entire world but not all are experiencing such forgiveness as not everybody believes in Jesus. In other words, not everybody has put their *faith* in what God has delivered through Jesus (*grace*). When we combine these two powerful elements, we can then see the manifestation of what God has done. As grace is a gift from God, we cannot ask for it, as we cannot ask for a gift but we have to receive it – such grace is constant and available unconditionally to everybody. Yet as previously noted, neither grace nor faith alone results in individual Salvation. Instead both elements must work collectively in order to produce the results of God's plan.

Ephesians 2:8 – '*For by grace you have been saved through faith and that not of yourselves; it is the gift of God.*'(NKJV)

Salvation is not received by grace alone or by faith but rather by grace through faith. One may not be able to benefit from God's wonderful plan if they do not apply faith in all that Jesus has already done. Indeed, the relationship is bilateral with responsibility on both sides – both God and human. Whilst an individual cannot lose or gain grace because it is divinely granted, because it does not depend on us, it is totally depends on God. They must observe their faith and put their unswerving trust in God in order to manifest His full power in their lives. When we understand the grace of God, we are able to develop a more intimate relationship with Him which is not based on individual performance but rather on His unmerited favour. When we stop relying in our performances and trust God, the result will be the grace will work for us.

Many believe that God will do and fail to appreciate that God has already done. This assertion is supported by an extract from Colossians 1:12, '*Giving thanks to the Father who has qualified us to be partakers of the inheritance of the saints in the light.*'(NKJV)

In this verse, the Holy Spirit, working through the apostle Paul, reiterates that it is God Himself who has qualified humankind to be His heirs and it is our responsibility to believe and to be thankful for every blessing that has already been bestowed. Similarly, whilst Jesus is quoted as saying "I am with you always, even to the end of the age"

(Matthew 28:20), many Christians still fail to appreciate what God has done and continue to call for His presence in their midst. Such individuals often believe that God's presence will not become manifest without their performance. In reality, however, His presence is always within every child of God. As such, because God dwells in the spirit of every child of God, believers are carrying the presence of God everywhere they go. Whilst we may not physically see or feel God's presence, we must be cognizant of the teachings of the Bible and be conscious that what has been written has already been accomplished. This is why faith appropriates of what God has already said and done through His son Jesus Christ.

When God met Moses, He told him "I AM WHO I AM, and thus shall thou say to the children of Israel, I AM has sent me to you" (Exodus 3:14). Through this use of present tense terminology, God hereby confirmed his continual existence and manifests to us through the faith that we use according to what God is for us. If we take God in the future, He cannot do anything now because He cannot violate man's will, we have to know that everything from God is already present in us.

According to the narrative of creation, God created everything that we see in five days and at the end of the sixth day He created man. This demonstrates that God anticipated the needs of man before such needs were realised. Such a scenario may be contrasted to one for example whereby God created man on the first day and created fish and vegetables for food on the third day. God knew in advance what would be necessary to sustain human life and He anticipated all such needs before even man came into existence. What was Adam prayer, I believe he was thanking and glorifying God that why it is easy to receive what we already have than looking for what we do not have.

God has created a blueprint for each and every one of us even before we were formed in our mother's womb. God had prepared and made everything ready for us; He had anticipated our lives even before our existence on earth. Our future had already been set out and the success that we see every day in our lives is not a surprise to God because He had in fact planned it. Our present life is a past to God, because He represents the beginning and the end of our lives. God put us on Earth so that we could start the course of our life that God had already finished - because God's work cannot be incomplete, and He cannot start anything without finishing it (Psalms 139:13-16). A useful analogy is an architect whom develops a plan for a property before subsequently passing this onto the builder. Whilst the owner may not rejoice and see the property until after its completion, for the architect this property is not new because he had already envisaged its construction and prepared for the property before its existence. In the present context, God Himself may be envisioned as the architect of our lives.

Whilst the death of Jesus occurred over two thousand years ago, his work and sacrifice were not just for the benefit of his contemporaries at the time but also for those who came later. As such, those who believe today receive the same blessings and benefits as those had believed before us. Indeed, God does not heal nor bless us today because this has already been accomplished. It is the responsibility of the individual to use their faith in order to obtain awareness of the sacrifices which have been made for humanity. Those who are presently suffering from a physical or mental ailment may ask how they have been healed. Faith involves believing what is invisible in order to bring this to a physical reality and one must not wait for the pain to disappear before accepting that you have been healed two thousand years ago. In Corinthians, Paul is quotes as sating "for we walk by faith, not by sight" (2 Corinthians 5:7). This reaffirms that faith is the spiritual eye which enables us to see our Salvation and the abundance of grace that we have received, I do not need first to see things physically but knowing that they exist in spiritual realm.

Salvation is made possible by the unmerited favour, I am not the one who produce grace but it is a gift of God. Individuals do not receive Salvation through their deeds but instead by believing and accepting the gift of Salvation. We do not merit nor deserve Salvation; it is impossible for man to replicate the works of perfection as performed by Jesus Christ. Humankind has been healed, delivered, blessed, protected, justified and sanctified by God's unmerited favour. All we can simply do is to apply our faith in all that was already done by grace.

2:
THE ORIGINS OF GRACE, FAITH AND SALVATION

2.1. The foundations of salvation beliefs

The Bible provides a framework for understanding that Salvation has been made possible by the love of God. Everything started with God and His love of all of creation and through his love He has decided to grant us an unmerited favour. We cannot talk and understand salvation without being conscious of the unconditional love of God.

Romans 5:8, 10 – *[8]But God demonstrates His own love toward us…[10]For if, while we were God's enemies, we were reconciled to him through the death of his Son…'* (NKJV)

The extract above demonstrates the unconditional love of God who has loved His creation from the moment it came into being despite the damage caused in our relationship with God through original sin. Indeed, it was not us who loved God but it was He who loved us and it was not us who looked for God but it was He who came to look for us. And it was God who came to reconcile humanity to Himself. Importantly, God did not love us because we were holy or because we were kind, but rather He loved us despite possessing full knowledge of our imperfections and flaws. In consequence, one must not accept the notion that good works are necessary in order for God to love them. God loved us and He came to us before mankind answered to the love of God. It is by His unconditional love that He has saved us in grace, and it is through faith that we accept Salvation which is a product of the love of God.

As grace is an unmerited favour, it does not depend on the actions of humankind but rather on the nature of God and His character. Whilst Jesus' death on the cross occurred over two thousand years ago, the grace which such a sacrifice bequeathed to humankind continues to exist up to the present day. God had already done everything before we came to know Him, now it is me to know and believe the love of God is the source of all blessings. Whilst many believers profess the word of God, they often believe that the blessings will manifest in the future this is the reason many do not experience them in present. Given the sacrifices already made for our benefit, when you are sick one must not say that "God will heal me" but rather that "I am healed because by the wounds of Jesus I was already healed two thousand years ago" (1 Peter 2:24). When we study this verse, Peter said we "were healed", this is already done and made possible to everyone. The prospect of Salvation came from the love and grace of God that was completed through the death and resurrection of Jesus Christ.

Titus 2:11 –*'For the grace of God that brings Salvation has appeared to all men.'* (NKJV)

This extract reiterates that Salvation was made available to all men through the grace of God and is not merited nor obtained but it is instead a free gift from God. Salvation as a package of many benefits that encompasses protection, victory, peace and all of God's blessings which was made possible through the suffering, death and resurrection of Jesus.

In reading the Bible, one must take into account the tense in which the text has been written – for example it has been said that God's grace has already been manifested, so it is a work that has already been completed. Salvation is made available to humankind through faith in what has already been accomplished. A new sacrifice is not required for the Salvation of each and every human being because Jesus died once and for the entire world. Jesus will not back to die on the cross again when someone want to be saved. The grace that is the source of salvation has already manifested for everyone without any exception, now everyone has to answer by believing that salvation. A similar line of reasoning may also be applied in the context of sickness whereby Jesus has already provided healing for all, but it is up to the individual to understand this and to apply their faith. It is important for us to discover what Jesus has done for us and believe it.

Salvation is a product of grace and this grace is in turn a product of the love of God. The plan for Salvation was made before the foundation of the world because God knows the end of everything before it has even begun. Prior to creation, God knew that man would diverge from Him through sin and He began preparing a solution to this problem before it occurred. The timing of Jesus' arrival was planned by God to deliver Salvation and to restore His original relationship with man. As set out in Genesis 3:15, God prophesied that "…I will put enmity between you and the woman, and between your offspring and hers; he will crush your head, and you will strike his heel. This prophecy was fulfilled on the cross, the devil was defeated and disarmed by Jesus and all those who believe in him are victorious as Jesus. Notwithstanding such prophesy, God made clothes from animal skin for Adam and his wife which were used to clothe them. Such an action evidences the plan of Salvation with the animal being a lamb that will take away the sins of the world and indeed Jesus was later sent as the Lamb of God for this purpose. John the Baptist first introduced Jesus in this context with the exclamation "behold, here is the Lamb of God who takes away the sins of the world" (John 1:29). Jesus' arrival represented the fulfilment of God's plans and the realisation of earlier prophesies which had predicted his birth, works and sacrifice for humanity.

Let me tell you that on the cross the head of the devil was crushed and today the devil does not have the head that he had before, the reason he has not the revelation of the cross and of the resurrection, he is the father of lies. If he has revelation, normally he should stop us believe in Jesus to not be saved.

The prospect of Salvation has already been made available to all of humankind and is not a reward that will be received in the future. We must recognise, accept and confess the gifts that God has already given us. Jesus did not die so that we can continue to be sick or be subject to the vices of the devil. The death and resurrection of Jesus transformed the life of all of humanity. Such a transformation is not manifested through our works but rather by knowing, believing and accepting God's grace. Unfortunately, many do not appreciate the sacrifices already made by God and instead put their trust in the performance of good works. We must first understand what Jesus has done for us and subsequently put our trust in his sacrifice in order for the power of the Holy Spirit to be manifested in our lives.

2.2. Grace is the person of Jesus Christ

Moses came with the law to reveal the sins of man however Jesus came to save humanity and to reveal the righteousness of God in man. That why the preaching of grace is the revelation of the righteousness of God to humankind. We have been saved by Jesus and also by God's grace as noted in the Bible, so we connect Jesus is the grace. In another way to say it, there is no salvation without Jesus and without grace.

John 1:18– *'For the law was given through Moses, but grace and truth came through Jesus Christ.' (NKJV)*

Interestingly, as set out in the extract above, whilst the law was relayed through the intermediary of Moses, grace and truth is a person who came to us in the form of Jesus Christ. He is the expression and the demonstration of the love of God - God so loved the world that He gave His only begotten Son. Grace was born by unconditional love and there is nothing that we can do that will increase or decrease God's love for us. For humankind, this means that we should centre our lives on His love, which represents our peace, our solution, our victory, our success and our blessing. Upon waking in the morning, one should breathe the freshness of this love and continue to thank God throughout the day, and this will result in a transformation of your life without your control. As the love of God is unconditional and constant, His grace is also unconditional and constant. We were once ineligible for Salvation and for the blessings of God but today we have been qualified before God - not because we deserved it or we have completed good works but instead simply because God loved us. Grace qualifies those who are disqualified and saves even the worst person. Jesus is the grace of God who came to Earth to represent us and to take our place.

On the cross, God did not see Jesus alone, but He instead saw Jesus as intertwined with humanity because the act of substitution/exchange was taking place on the cross.

Matthew 27:46 states 'And about the ninth hour Jesus cried out with a loud voice saying, "Eli, Eli, lama sabachthani?" That is, My God, My God, why have You forsaken me? If one is to read the four gospels, it will be noted that this was the first time that Jesus called his Father in the name of God because he had previously always called Him Father according to their relationship. On the cross, Jesus took the place of all of humanity (whom was sinful) and humanity took the place of Jesus (who was righteous). Consequently, at this time, Jesus could not call God his Father because he became sin and the world who became righteous in Jesus' position could now call God its Father. Whilst Jesus cried out "My God, why have you forsaken me?" humankind could exclaim "My Father, why have you accepted me?"

No one deserved to be accepted by God because at this time, all Jews and nations without exception were condemned. It is through God's will and choice that we were accepted and blessed. We do not deserve, nor do we obtain the grace of God through good works, but it is instead a free gift. Jesus was sacrificed by God for the Salvation of the entire world and all that he has accomplished is may be freely received by all. Grace came to serve us, to strengthen our resolve and enable us to combat all of the negative influences. Grace came to restore man back to his position before original sin and back to his relationship of love with God for the will of God that is in heavens to be done on earth. Grace came to give human the power to dominate over the evil.

2.3. Grace is for everybody

There are a number of passages in the Bible which reaffirm that God's plan is for all of humanity and not just for selected individuals. As such, it encompasses all races, classes, socio-economic groups in addition to any other anthropogenic division. All have sinned, the word "all" includes everybody, from the first Adam to the last person who will be born. And these "all" who have sinned have been justified freely by the grace of God (Romans 3:23-24). Following the sacrifice on the cross, God has perceived the world through the work accomplished by His son and holds no enmity, however many still hold enmity towards God and have not yet accepted Salvation through Jesus Christ. God has solved the conflict which existed between Himself and the world however not everybody has benefitted from this resolution because not everybody believes in Jesus.

Titus 2:11 –*'For the grace of God that brings Salvation has appeared to all men.' (NKJV)*

It has previously been asserted that grace alone does not save, but rather it must be accepted by faith. Nonetheless, God loves everybody and his plan for those who are and who will be on Earth has been realised. The extract from Titus reiterates that the grace of God, which is the source of Salvation, has already been manifested for all of humanity without exception. God is not unjust and does not love certain individuals whilst disliking others. Humankind has the responsibility to respond through faith to such grace in order to obtain the benefits of Salvation. Jesus, who is the grace of God, did not die for certain individuals but for all of humanity. We are the receivers of this grace and God as the giver. One may ask, "If God has already healed everybody, why I am not healed or why have many people not been saved?" In reality however, Jesus is the source of protection, grace, healing and victory for all and this has been manifested. In other side each one of us we have the responsibility to receive that by faith.

1 John 2:2 – *'And He himself is the propitiation for our sins, and not for ours only but also for the whole world.'(NKJV)*

The work of Jesus made possible the Salvation of all of humanity – therefore in the mind of God all have been forgiven and saved. When an individual accepts Jesus Christ into their life, God does not forgive them in that moment because all their sins were already forgiven on the cross. However, such forgiveness becomes a reality in the life of the person on the day that they believe and accept the sacrifice of Jesus.

2.4. Faith as imparted by God

There are two types of faith - God's faith and a human's faith. A human's faith consists of first seeing the sign or tangible thing before being willing to accept its existence whilst that of God involves accepting and receiving the spiritual blessing before physically witnessing the palpable thing. Man cannot be saved by human faith because the things of God are first spiritual before they are manifest physically. Indeed, Romans 12:3 stipulates that 'God hath dealt to every man the measure of faith.' Notable here is use of the term 'the measure' as opposed to 'a measure' – implying that we have all received the requisite quantity and quality of faith from God. Similar sentiments were expressed by the apostle Peter who explained that we have all obtained precious faith (2 Peter 1:1). Such faith belongs to God and was given to humankind as a means to connect ourselves to His grace in order to be saved and to experience all that He has prepared for us.

When someone listen the good news of Jesus Christ, the Holy Spirit convinces the individual to believe and to accept Jesus in their heart. When God sees in an individual a desire and a conviction to change, God gives the individual the portion of His faith required for them to access Salvation. Those who believe receive the same type and measure of faith as those who came before and those who will believe later and is sufficient to guide the individual through their Christian life.

Luke 17:6 recounts an occasion whereby one day the disciples asked Jesus to increase their faith. Jesus 'response was that an increase in faith was not necessary because the measure of faith already granted was sufficient to perform miracles. Simply, we need to focus and to use the faith that God has given us. We have the same faith that Jesus had but he was using it in every situation without doubt and without fear because he knew who he was and what he had been gifted. God has given us faith for us to appropriate on the provision of blessing that we have in Christ. Grace is the responsibility of God and faith is the responsibility of man. Through the provision of grace, God had anticipated everything which was required for our lives whereas faith is a mechanism for humankind to absorb all that has been provided by grace. As such, God has already provided us with healing before sickness has even occurred and He has given us the abundance of everything before we identified a need.

The human body has five senses (touch, smell, taste, sight and sound) which are important for the physical life of day to day functioning however there is also a sixth sense which God has given us that connects us to the spiritual realm. Adam and Eve experienced this sense as they were naked, but they could not perceive their nakedness. Indeed, God wants us to live with this sense which sees with the eyes of the heart -in other words the eyes of faith. Faith provides individuals with affirmation of the things that their physical eyes cannot see - hence why God exclaimed that "...the righteous man shall live by faith." (Romans 1:17)

2.5. The Cross and the Resurrection

The sacrifice of Jesus on the cross provided humanity with the entrance to a new life through the New Covenant. Jesus is both the founder and the foundation of

Christianity because his death made possible new life for all of humanity. Whilst the devil had deceived the first man with his wife to obtain their authority but through the sacrifice of Jesus on the cross the devil was disarmed and made powerless. The devil operates by blinding people's intelligence and rendering them ignorant so that he is able to control them. Because what we do not know cannot work for us. The devil knows that he cannot touch a child of God and he has therefore introduced many false doctrines in order to hide the good news of grace to the children of God because he knows that when we have knowledge of the truth we will live the fullness of God's life (2 Corinthians 4:4).

The cross is the place where Jesus forgave all of our sins, healed us and delivered us however prior to his death humanity continued to exist in the nature of original sin and subject to the influence of the devil. Upon Jesus' death, we died with the sinful nature that we had and we were buried with him and the sin nature was destroyed, and through the resurrection humankind received a new spirit that is more powerful than the devil and no longer controlled by his influence.

In 1 Corinthians 15:1, Paul said "…I want to remind you of the gospel I preached to you" and in Corinthians 15:3-4 he notes that Christ died for our sins and was buried and raised on the third day. Broadly then, the Apostle Paul is explaining that the proclamation of the good news is centred on the cross and on the resurrection of Jesus and thereby presents a Christocentric. The cross of Jesus is the expression of the unconditional love of God because He has accepted to humble Himself to accept death for the purpose to save all humanity.

The sacrifice of Jesus on the cross is a free offer made available to all which took away defeat and sickness and made it possible for humankind to be victorious and to live in divine health. The cross has taken away the curse of all and to receive blessing. In considering the devil as a standalone figure, he appears powerful however in the context of the sacrifice on the cross he is weak and has been defeated.

One cannot contemplate the privileges that have been received by the children of God without first understanding the power of the cross and the resurrection. When an individual believes and accepts Jesus into their life, the reality of the new birth becomes a truth. Through the resurrection, our lives were transformed, and we became new creatures that never existed before. This aligns with the teachings as set out in Galatians that what count is being a new creation (Galatians 6:15). Those who were sinful, cursed, separated from God and possessed by the devil died and buried with Jesus. Children of God did not come from the cross but instead came from God and were born from above that is made possible by the resurrection with Jesus.

Given knowledge of these facts, it is now the responsibility of the individual to understand them, believe them and, through faith, to accept God's presence in their lives. It is through the resurrection that we have now been re-seated together with Jesus in heaven. According to the apostle Paul, a failure to understand Jesus' work on the cross and his resurrection prevents the believer from benefitting from the intended outcomes of these events. Consequently, preaching the good news of the abundance of grace should not only focus upon the cross but also upon the realisation of new life through Jesus' resurrection. It also means that our faith should be founded on the cross and the resurrection and not simply on our physical works. Indeed, it is important to see and to interpret every situation in light of the cross and resurrection. This sacrificial focus serves to differentiate Christianity from other faiths and in fact it may be argued that Christianity is not a religion but is in fact the actual life of God in all those who have been saved. Jesus came to give his life for humanity by his suffering, death and resurrection.

Unfortunately, many individuals are more pre-occupied with their own circumstances rather than the life of God which exists within them. However, one must not let circumstances dictate their faith but should instead use faith to dictate their circumstances. Know that Jesus made the ultimate sacrifice to overcome the original sin which had been instigated by Adam. Through his work on the cross and his resurrection, Jesus made us free and it is important for us to be conscious of the deliverance, justification and life of God that we are living. All that was previously wrong with the old nature of humanity is not applicable as our spirits have been born again through the resurrection. It is important for believers to have a comprehensive understanding of God's grace and sacrifice for us as possessing an inadequate knowledge of faith may otherwise lead individuals to lead a wrong life.

3:
RENEWAL OF THE MIND

3.1. New person with a new programme

When an individual becomes a child of God, they become a brand-new person in his spirit but also need to renew the programme of their soul. Prior to the resurrection, every child of God was a sinner and living with an internal programme that was afflicted with the impacts of original sin. Old programme is a product of the old nature, the environment, the culture and even the education and also the believe system. Whilst the Bible tells us that our old sinful nature was crucified with Jesus and our spirit transformed through his resurrection, the soul and the body continue to exist as before. In order to align the body, soul and spirit, it is necessary to delete the sinful programme in our minds and to replace this with a completely new programme which is a complex process occurring over a period of time. If a child of God fails to change the way that they think, speak, believe and see themselves, they will be unable to harness the full power of God and His blessings will not be completely manifested in their life. As it is known that the old man does not exist anymore but they have left an old programme that continue to dictate the everyday life.

Such an assertion is supported by the text of Philippians 4:8 which may be interpreted as whatever things are true, noble, just, pure and lovely should be meditated upon and therefore be the object of the mind of the child of God because our mental thoughts has the power to control our lives. Unfortunately, many children of God continue to speak, think, and behave and to live in a manner analogous to that of the old sinful life. In order to re-write out existing sinful programme, we must re-educate our minds according to the person that we are in Christ. We are a new being in spirit through the born again act, we need to live with a new programme according to the person we are in Christ.

It is important to control the environment in which we live, who we spend our time with and who we listen to. If we do not discipline ourselves, we will not be able tore-write the old programme because a change in outcomes results from a change in the mind. A revised programme will not be implemented automatically because it requires personal discipline. There are a significant number of negative influences in the modern world and this can often cause individuals to lose hope and to experience fear. A useful analogy is a home computer - when you have a computer which functions with an old program or operating system, you need to delete the old version and replace it with a new one. You cannot mix conflicting programmes because neither will work.

Changing one's mindset is a significant undertaking and although transformation of the spirit occurs immediately at the moment when a person believes and receives Jesus

Christ into their lives, changing of the soul (mind, conscious, mentality, emotion etc.) is a process. As we know that every change comes from a change.

The soul is the centre point between the spirit and the body; the spirit does not control the body directly, but the soul does. If the spirit could affect our physical behaviours directly, it would be easy for God's grace within us to change our physical lives. The soul serves as the mediator between spirit and body, when our souls and spirit are aligned with the same understanding, the body will be impacted by the force of this knowledge because the majority overrules the minority.

The mind places a crucial function in the manifestation of the benefits of individual Salvation. Whilst many are happy to undertake good time of prayers but they often forget to cultivate and to harness the power of the mind and this opens up the possibility of the negativity to get access. One may consider this analogous to closing the doors in a house to prevent insect infestation whilst leaving a window open. The devil operates by bringing negativity into an individual's life - he cannot control a person if he does not first change their mind.

Indeed, when the devil sought to tempt Adam and Eve, he succeeded by controlling their mind and encouraging them to go against what God had told them. He spoke to them about the tree of the knowledge of good and evil and changed their attitudes and perceptions towards the tree. Whilst the tree had existed for some time, Adam and Eve had noticed it but had never otherwise thought about it. The devil cannot tempt you if your mind has not yet thought about something. Similarly, one may hear about the symptom of a disease for the first time that you never know or thought about. One day you have some feelings in the body, the mind beginning to focus upon such a symptom by telling you that is the beginning of that sickness, many have experienced the beginning of the disease because what they have downloaded in their mind. Although the disease may have been in your body already, if you had never known and thought about it, it may not have had an impact on you.

Proverbs 23:7 – *'For as he thinks in his heart, so is he…'* (NKJV)

If you consider yourself as poor, eventually this will be realised. In contrast, if you invest the time in listening and seeing, you will realise that you have the facility to build your thought. The ears and eyes provide the entrance to your thoughts and the mouth is the expression of such. What a person thinks will be realised through their words and actions – this is why the mind has the power to affect your daily existence. A child of God must evidence discipline and not give their ears to just anybody – rather they must understand and control exactly what their body hears. The mind is subject to the influences to which it is exposed and commands the body to enact what is programmed in it. As such, the mind is like a telecommunications exchange and all phone calls must first go first through the exchange to be directed to the destination. Do not give even one minute to the devil otherwise he will instil bad thoughts and ideas in you.

3.2. Transformation by the renewing of the Mind

The Holy Spirit operates in the transformation of children of God and helps to protect the individual from negative worldly influences but he accentuates that the transformation of the physical activities is made possible by the principle of renewal of the mind. Our minds are so powerful that they can limit the manifestation of God's power. Paul

Humans exist as a spirit; they have a soul and are physically represented in a body. Before to their rebirth in Jesus, an individual existed within the devil's empire and was subject to the influence of darkness. The devil possesses their spirit and their soul cannot do anything other than what the devil has already programmed into them. The nature of such individuals is one of sin and their actions and reactions are dictated by malevolence. One may compare such a scenario to that of a computer which cannot run any another program apart from those that have already been installed onto it. When a person is born again, their body and soul remain constant however their spirit undergoes a fundamental transformation. The person who existed before is no longer because they have been crucified and buried with Jesus. At this point, the devil which was commanding the individual to do evil is now gone and the person has become a new creature which has never existed before. The Bible tells us that if anyone is in Christ, he is a new creation, notes that the Bible emphases that "old things" have passed away, behold (means: see-evidence), "all things" have become news. This is not a theory but a truth of every child of God life.

Romans 12:2 teaches us to "…not conform to the pattern of the world but be transformed by renewing the mind…" We have a choice in this regard and must not submit to the devil or the negative influences in the world if we wish to fully experience the will of God. Normally, the situation has not the power to control my life but it is my choice of submitting to it or to see it in the light of what the Lord Jesus has fulfilled.

The Greek word for 'transform' is 'metamorphoo' and is analogous to the English word 'metamorphosis' which means a change of nature or character. A frequently cited example from the natural world is when a caterpillar becomes a butterfly. But how cans such a transformation of life can be achieved? It is via a renewal of the mind.

Upon rebirth, the spirit is transformed into a perfect form which enables the individual to fully embrace the life of God in all areas of life through the renewal of the mind. One has the power to change negative situations by seeing and confessing the opposite viewpoint. For example, one may consult a doctor who tells you that you are developing a sickness in the body. In such situations, one must respond "thank you for your diagnostic; however I will never suffer from this sickness." Whilst the doctor may be relaying the truth, your faith and your positive mind will destroy that sickness. 'Let God be true, and every human being a liar…' (Romans 3:4). Whilst every fact can be changed, truth cannot change - sickness and existential problem may be facts but they are not a truth, however the truth is what Jesus has already done.

For example, sickle cell anaemia is an abnormality of the blood; however through renewal of the mind, one can mitigate and even prevent the disorder from impacting upon day to day life. The change is possible, either the abnormality disappears or it is still there but does not cause you a health problem anymore. This is because you have already been healed by Jesus two thousand years ago and you have a divine health in you. You are not poor and seeking to prosper - you are prosperous, but the devil is trying to lie to you that you are poor. You are not a sinner who is trying to be saint - you are already a saint and the devil is trying to convince you otherwise. The devil is trying to push you to misread the word of God; he is working with his negative influence. Consequently, we must 'cast down every high thing that exalts itself against the knowledge of God and bring every thought into captivity to the obedience of Christ' (2 Corinthians 10:5). Following Jesus' resurrection, the devil yields no power, however he is still able to use lies to deceive people. If one possesses knowledge of the truth, the truth will make them free and victorious. In this time of grace, the authority of God is within man to give provide order and to resist all negative influence. Knowledge of the gospel is powerful means of renewing our mind because the word of God is a mirror which allows us to see who we are and what we have in Christ. What we hear and what we see have the capacity to change our minds and therefore we should be vigilant in all that we do. The devil attacks the truth that you know and try to send to you wrong knowledge, because wrong knowledge brings to wrong believing and wrong believing brings to wrong living.

3.3. The battle is in the Mind

In reality, our battle takes place in our mind because our mind operates in accordance to the thoughts which we let enter. In this context, it is useful to know what is exactly about spiritual warfare and we have to know that the devil and demons were defeated and disarmed (they are powerless) on the cross. Luke 10:19 teaches us that "Nothing shall by any means hurt you." Since the time you have been saved, there is no creature that can destroy or hurt you. The devil and his demons are powerless, they are beneath your feet and you are seated in the heavenly place with Christ. If one is able to change their mind, then they can live the reality of a victorious life. Do not waste time or energy focusing on demons but we need to focus on Jesus and in what he has accomplished for us. When you talk more about a person, you are lifting them up and glorifying them and it is a way you get his attention to come to you. Fill your mind with all that we have received in Christ because all that Jesus has fulfilled on the cross and through his resurrection is the reality of our life. The demons which we encounter today are the same as those which existed before the cross, but they no longer have the power that they once possessed. Jesus has disarmed them and triumphed over them on the cross. Today the devil with his demons has zero, zero power and you are not in the same position and same level with them; they are under your feet. In focusing more on Jesus and what he has fulfilled through his death and resurrection, we open the door to the manifestation of blessings that we have received.

The devil knows that he has no power to touch a child of God; however he uses a cascade of lies in order to deceive many. The devil wants to separate the mind from the spirit in order to control them. He sends us false information to challenge our minds and prevent us from knowing the good news of Jesus. He attacks the good news that we receive because he knows that the more knowledge of truth we possess, the less he is able to touch us. This is reaffirmed in Matthew 13:19 which teach us that when we listen to the word of God and do not understand it, the devil comes to take away that which was sown in us. The truth that we do not know does not work in us, only the truth that we do know is capable of setting us free. It is important to recognise that there is no lie without truth because every lie is the truth deformed. The devil came to Adam and Eve with a distorted version of the word of God and he also came to Jesus with what God the Father had said at the River Jordan as he was seeking to put Jesus in doubt of his identity. Such mechanisms of deception are the same as those used against humankind today and indeed the twenty first century has provided the devil which many technological doors to seduce people with false doctrines.

The devil imparts negative thoughts into our mind which are contrary to the word of God and blind us to the benefits that the good news gives us. Knowledge of the good news of Jesus Christ will build up our awareness of the beauty of grace. One must keep a positive mind through knowledge of the truth and not allow negative information to take root. One must continue to believe in the person that they are in Christ even when facing difficulties and to recognise the power of disciplined ways of thinking. What people put in their mind has the power to control their life and actions. As the man think in the heart, so they are.

The devil has established temptations and mechanisms to obtain influence over individuals however God has given us His armour to overcome. As previously noted, the devil has no power over a child of God without the person first accepting his lie and his system of mind control. Our mind receives everything that comes from external senses and directs it towards bodily action -hence why it is important to fortify our minds with all that is positive and truth of the gospel. For example, one may listen to a message suggesting that your life is not going very well because you are cursed. If you were to allow such a message to enter your mind, every time something is not going well in life, your mind will tell you that you are cursed because that is the linkage which you have created. Nothing will work for you because the mind is dictating to you that you are cursed. Furthermore, when a child of God is mentally negative, their faith will also not as function well because the eyes of one's faith must see what they believe.

One of the reasons for the longevity of Adam and Eve and other earlier Biblical characters is because their mind had not yet received information about death and sickness. Nobody had taught them about the symptoms of sickness or poverty and also, they didn't know about death or other negative things. When Adam experienced a headache for the first time, I believe that he was intrigued as to what the problem was. It took time for the devil to affect their mind in a negative way. In modern times, whilst the development of technology has had many important benefits, it also serves to transmit negative information and can unfortunately lead people to follow the wrong path or even to commit self-harm or suicide based upon the information they have been exposed to and allowed to infiltrate into their mind.

3.4. The mentality in the Kingdom of God

The term 'mentality' refers to our usual way of thinking, which in turn impacts upon our beliefs and actions. We often do things out of habit or think in certain ways based upon what we have learned through teaching and experience. It is important to remain vigilant and to cross check information which we receive as repeated information or repeated practices can be downloaded into our subconscious. And depending on the circumstances, can have a negative impact upon our mentality and well being. As such the concept of 'mentality' is central to the process of changing one's life. What differentiates people is the way that they think, speak, perceive a situation and, perhaps most importantly of all, the way that they see themselves. Knowing that, everything that has been downloaded in our subconscious becomes a master to control our thought and the external life.

Galatians 4:1 states that '…the heir, as long as he is a child, does not differ at all from a slave, though he is master of all.' In this verse, there is identified a child, due to legally position of inherit material goods, and also the verse identifies that the child is the master of all and there is a slave who serve the master. In Greek, the child as included in this verse is described by the word 'nepios'- meaning an immature child. As the heir is not yet at the age of maturity, he will not be able to benefit from their inherent privilege until they reach the age of legal recognition. Whilst everything in their home technically belongs to them, they are in essence of no higher status than a slave. Many children of God may be considered to be in a state of immaturity as they have no yet recognised the blessings which have been provided for them or they do not know who they are and what they posess in their born again spirit. Indeed, the Bible teaches us that a child of God is an heir and a co-heir with Christ, but through a lack of maturity and appreciation of what Jesus Christ has fulfilled for them, many are effectively still living with a slave mentality. In order to fully benefit from God's blessings, children of God must change their mentality, free themselves from distractions and use their faith to impact their world. This type of child of God needs the teachings of the gospel of Jesus for the purpose of growing and become mature. As the apostle Paul said in Corinthians 13:11, 'When I was a child, I talked like a child, I thought like a child, I reasoned like a child. When I became a man, I put the ways of childhood behind me.'

God has delivered us from the power of darkness and brought us into the Kingdom of His Son (Colossians 1:13) - we are citizens of God's kingdom, our way of speaking and thinking must to be different to those imparting a negative influence upon the world. In the Kingdom of God, one must take the time to reflect and to adopt a positive mentality because we know that life and death are in the power of tongue. We must recognise that we have been blessed with God's grace and thank the Lord – even though His blessings are not seen first physically evident to us but we are fully convinced that we are really blessed. In the Kingdom of God, we live by faith which in turn allows the power of God to be truly manifest in the physical reality. Through his death and resurrection, Jesus has disarmed the devil, taken away the curse of humanity and restored our relationship with God. The realisation of such benefits is fulfilled by the Holy Spirit who dwells in the spirit of all believers. Collectively, these truths provide a positive mentality through the understanding that everything has been accomplished. Every child of God is a new person in Christ who lives in a new reality; however one must still continue to assess and to develop their mentality in order to live in accordance with the life that has been prescribed for us in the Kingdom of God. The Kingdom of God is established to work with principles and knowing our rights and faith are one of those principles.

Ephesians 4:24 teaches us that we must '…put on the new man which was created according to God, in true righteousness and holiness.' The idea is like putting on clothes on the body and when you look at the person you do not see the body but the clothes. In simple terms, this means that our exterior person must reflect our new internal nature in Christ through our way of living and actions the way in which we interact with people on a day to day basis. A positive mentality and a good attitude must become a fundamental tenet of our everyday lives. A child of God is living the life of God (Greek: Zoe) and the life of God is not natural but supernatural and this makes that every child of God is not natural but supernatural.

4:
WORKS AND GRACE

4.1. Grace as an unmerited favour

Jesus taught us that nobody uses a piece of un-shrunken cloth to mend an old coat and no one pours new wine in the old wineskins (Matthew 9:16). Such teachings were referring to the fact that the works of the law and grace cannot be mixed - if one seeks to pursue both then there will be a sub-optimal outcome. We are now living under the time of grace as the law was fulfilled by Jesus on the cross. The law was based upon the physical works that man has to do whereas grace is based upon what Jesus has done already. This is why our trust must be solely placed in what God has done for us already and not in what we are going to do through our own actions. The mentality under the law uses the verb "to do" whereas under the grace uses the verb "to believe" and "to receive".

Under the dispensation of grace, whilst there is a place for both God's grace and the performance of good works, it is important to recognise that grace is not obtained by what we do but it is instead an unmerited favour. The goodness of God is more powerful than our works. Unfortunately, many of God's children ultimately end up disappointed because they rely more on what they do for God instead recognising what God has already done for them. Our relationship with God is based upon His unconditional love and not upon our works of merit. The concept of works incorporates a range of behaviours including going to church, giving offerings, fasting, reading the Bible, serving the community and so forth. Whilst such activities enable us to receive what God has given us and resist the devil, as it is known that God has loved us before us to perform good works.

Galatians 2:16– *'Know that a person is not justified by the works of the law, but by faith in Jesus Christ.' (NKJV)*

Romans 11:6– *'And if by grace, then it is no longer of works; otherwise grace is no longer grace. But if it is of works, it is no longer grace; otherwise work is no longer work.' (NKJV)*

Grace is an unmerited favour which was made possible by the unconditional love of God. Abraham was justified by faith when he believed God and not by the works he performed - as we know he was not under the dispensation of law because he has lived before the law was given. Abraham was able to prosper because he focused upon the love of God as he lived under in the shadow of grace under the dispensation of conscious. As such, it was not by fasting or any of the other typically recognised works that Abraham was blessed - but rather it was by faith in what God told and promised him.

Before the death and the resurrection of Jesus, blessing was conditional – in other words one must obey the law in order to receive God's blessing – otherwise you will be cursed, under the law God was depending on what man was doing. When you perform well you will receive good and when you perform bad you will get bad. When reading Exodus 20, the law was set out in the Ten Commandments, written on stone tablets, which prohibited and prescribed certain behaviours by humankind. For example, 'thou shall not murder' and 'thou shall have no other gods before me'. As such the outcome, and acceptance by God, was fundamentally dependent upon individual performance.

In contrast, the receipt of grace does not depend upon the deeds of man but rather upon what Jesus has already done on the cross and through his resurrection. This represents a fundamental shift in the relationship between God and humanity and our responsibility is now to believe and to accept what has been done in our place rather than to demonstrate our worth via physical works. This is demonstrated by the literary shift in emphasis from 'Thou shall' (Exodus 20:1-17) to 'I will' (Hebrew 8:10-12) which signifies that it is not man doing the work anymore but rather it is God Himself who is working. Religion places the emphasis upon the individual works of man whereas Christianity emphasises what Jesus has already done.

Hebrew 8:10-12 -*'For this is the covenant that I will make with the house of Israel after those days, says the Lord: I will put My laws in their mind and write them on their hearts…' (NKJV)*

God has loved, blessed and healed us before we knew Him and has forgiven our sins before we came to be His children. Everything is done by God's choice and is motivated by the nature of His love – this is why we must be cognizant of His unmerited favour. Everything we do does not change God's position towards us but rather it changes our position in relation to God. We do not deserve the love and grace of God because everything that we have received from Him is a gracious free gift. He loves us unconditionally and has also given us unconditional grace - it is up to the individual to live this love and grace to the extent that they desire. Consider a situation whereby you are near to a river and in need of water – in such circumstances you will draw as much water as you need. If you are in need of water at home, you would not contact the water company to send you the quantity of water that you need but instead you would simply open the tap and draw all that you need. Similarly, we do not ask for the love and grace of God, they are freely available to us and we simply need to receive them in the quantity that we want.

Ephesians 3:18-19 -*'May be able to comprehend with all saints what is the width and length and depth and height, to know the love of Christ which passes knowledge; that you may be filled with all the fullness of God.' (NKJV)*

The focus of the extract above is about comprehending the love of Christ which is made possible through the indwelling of the spirit and the rooting and grounding of humankind in love. The use of the term 'all saints' confirms that such understanding is not reserved only for certain individuals but is available to each of us. The love of God has no limits and no dimensions and can be understood through knowledge of the revelation. Those who lack an understanding of the revelation live a superficial life of God's love. A further important section in the above passage is 'to know the love of Christ which passes knowledge...'

'To know' is a verb which is derived from the Greek word 'Ginosko' and as a verb expresses action, it can be taken to mean 'to have experienced knowledge. 'Knowledge' similarly comes from the Greek word 'Gnosis' and may be interpreted as 'theory knowledge.' Paul teaches us that we need to be rooted in the love of God, it is not only by saying that God loves me but it has to become the experience of life. This is the attitude of everyday life rather than verbal expression. A positive attitude focused upon the love of God enables us to manifest His fullness in our lives. If a child of God does not live a life filled with the fullness of God's presence, it means that they have not experienced of the love of God.

Under the law as set out in the Old Testament, it was man who had to first evidence love towards God before God in turn loved him, however but under grace it was God who first loved us. One cannot love God solely though their own actions but instead must know Him and accept His unconditional love. This is the reason many are not able to love others because of lack of understanding how much God loves them. You cannot give what you do not have.

4.2. The Role of Good Works

The performance of good works does not change the attitude of God towards us, but it does change our attitudes towards God. Nothing can increase or decrease God's love or the grace that he has given us. Whilst physical actions are an important element of the Christian faith, it is the motivation and purpose behind such actions will determined the result. One should not do good deeds solely in the pursuit of God's love or acceptance. God does not love us on the basis of the number of times that we pray or fast – His love is unconditional, and He has accepted us for entry into His Kingdom is His choice and will.

Many believers make the common error of putting their faith in what they do. They may pray and fast however they do not fully cultivate God's blessings because they possess the wrong motivations and as such have been deceived by the devil. For example, the devil may convince you that if you forget to read the Bible God will not love you. In such circumstances, it is important to remember that God loves you unconditionally and His love does not depend upon your deeds. If you forget to read the Bible, God will continue to love you as His love is constant but in fact, you read the Bible to know your rights and to have knowledge regarding your life in Christ. In contrast, if a child of God were to say, "I want to fast for twenty days in order for God to heal me of this disease", they are not using their faith in the work of Jesus instead and they are using faith as the basis of their healing. Faith always functions in accordance with what Jesus has already done and not what we do. Knowing what the Lord Jesus has done is the key of the healing and success in life.

Faith functions in conjunction with grace - as grace is the abundance of all that God has done through Jesus. In other words, faith only appropriates what was done by Jesus because faith does not create anything new. Our good works are acts of faith which manifest what we already have in spirit. Good works provide a means of preventing the devil from obtaining access in our lives. We are rewarded in our life on earth and we will also be rewarded again in heaven through our good works and the good performances protect the relationship with others. Whilst the world is often organised on the basis of a meritocracy, Christianity is based on Jesus' merits alone. We cannot win or obtain entitlement to the blessings of God, but we instead already possess them through His grace. We do not deserve to be children of God and Jesus did not deserve to suffer and die on the cross. That is the reason why we must give thanks to the Father who has pre-qualified us to receive His blessings. A failure to understand the grace of God often results in confusion in the lives of believers and indeed many practice-based religious traditions can also be considered to have misinterpreted the grace of God.

1 Peter 2:24 -*'Who Himself bore our sins in His own body on the tree, that we, having died to sins, might live for righteousness - by whose stripes you were healed.' (NKJV)*

This extract does not say that we will be healed through our own actions such as by fasting, but instead notes that we have already been healed through the stripes of Jesus. Such a blessing has already been received and has not been postponed to a point of future entitlement. One must accept that any sickness which you are feeling has already been healed and you will receive such benefits by confessing that you are in good health. Our faith must be focused on it is already done than it will be done. Upon confession, every human sickness that you could feel has no root anymore - it is superficial. God healed us before we even came into the world and the devil seeks to deceive us by convincing us that we must take physical action in order to be healed. The root of every negative influence was the nature of the first Adam and Jesus became that nature on the cross to cut the root and set people free.

After obtaining an awareness of God's love, we are motivated to undertake good works. We may also invest additional time in prayer as it serves to edify us and develop our relationship with God. As previously noted, good works serve as a defence against the devil and prevent him from obtaining a controlling influence in our lives. Yet whilst the performance of good works is an integral part of the Christian life, it is more important to have honest motivations and a good attitude. One must also take care to not put all of their faith in those good works but instead to put their faith in what is already done by Jesus on the cross and through his resurrection. Indeed, the Apostle Paul has reiterated that we must not put our trust in our performances but instead in the goodness of God. The truth is that regardless of the number of good works that we undertake, it will not be sufficient to produce Salvation because Salvation is the product of the love of God. If you consider that your life is not going well, stop, reflect and put all of your trust in Jesus and in what he has accomplished.

4.3. God is the Provider and I am the receiver

God the Father by His love has given us everything through the sacrifice of His son Jesus Christ. Jesus is the gift that God bequeathed for the Salvation of humanity and through this offering we have received all gifts. In John 4:10, Jesus said to the Samaritan "If you knew the gift of God, and who it is who says to you, 'Give Me a drink,' you would have asked Him, and He would have given you living water." God is our source and He has made grace to all, even those often condemned by society. Whilst in the Old Testament it was humankind giving to God through obedience of the commandments and the performance of good works, but under grace it is now God who has given to humankind through the sacrifice of his son and the provision of grace. Jesus is the abundance of everything and whoever believes in him and receives him will share in this abundance. Law came to receive from man but grace came to serve humanity as it is written that we have all received from his fullness grace upon grace.

Matthew 11:28 – *'Come to Me, all you who labor and are heavy laden, and I will give you rest.'(NKJV)*

The requirement to justify oneself in the time of the Old Testament was a burden that no one was able to bear because man had already been separated from God as a result of the original sin. James 2:10 states, for whoever shall keep the whole law, and yet stumble in one point, he is guilty of all. Jesus came to Earth in order to relieve humankind of the obligations that they could not fulfil. Jesus came to take our place and to fulfil what we were unable to do. During his time on Earth, Christ walked in our name and did everything for us, thereby acting as a substitute. Just as God rested on the seventh day after the creation, Jesus went to the cross in order to bring us into this rest. He has obeyed the law on our behalf and our faith in him renders us obedient children. Entry into the Kingdom of God is made possible through faith and we must live our daily Christian life in faith (Hebrew 4:3).

It has previously been explained that all have not yet been saved as not everybody believes in Jesus Christ and accepts him as their saviour. The problem is not with the giver but rather with the receiver. Today, many ask God to stretch out His hand and to bless them because they do not know that His hand is permanently with them in the form of the Holy Spirit. Others may pray for God to come down to us, or to be with us, without understanding that God will not appear in their midst because He is already with us. Hebrew 13:5 notes how God said that "I will not leave nor forsake you" and in Matthew 28:20, Jesus is quoted as saying "And behold, I am with you always, to the end of the age."

We receive everything of God by faith and not by emotions or feelings. Whilst faith is not an emotion, it can produce emotion. God is present wherever we gather in His name and we must thank God for his presence in our lives and express a desire through faith for his blessings to be manifested in our lives.

2 Peter 1:3-4 –*'His divine power has given to us all things that pertain to life and godliness…' (NKJV)*

Whilst every child of God possesses the capacity for faith which has been granted to them, they often fail to understand the way in which faith operates and also what God the Father has already done for us through the sacrifice of His son, Jesus. Faith cannot function on what we do not know. Prior to entering into the world, God prepared a better and a blessed course for each one of us. He is the alpha and omega who starts and ends our lives and has placed us on Earth with His blessings and His grace. If one were to read the epistle to the Ephesians for example, it would be noted that the tone of this letter focuses more upon the past and in particular the revelation that everything has already been done.

Peter 1:3 states that '…His divine power has given to us all things that pertain to life and godliness, through the knowledge of Him who called us by glory and virtue…' Our born again spirits have been abundantly filled with everything that we need and 'through the knowledge of Him' we become partakers of His divine nature. Being partaker with God means we are working in association with Him, as all His power is in the believer. Notice this verse says that "all things" are in the believer spirit and this is the reason we thank Him. One may again recall the analogy of the household tap whereby we have all the facilities required and simply need to draw the quantity of water - or in this case, God's gifts which we desire. Children of God are complete in Spirit (Colossians 2:10) and faith enables us to manifest what is in the spirit because we do not walk according to what we see but by faith. One must believe that they are already richly blessed because it is the will of God for us to prosper in all areas of our lives. Faith is crucial as it enables children of God to appropriate all of the things that God has already prepared for them.

4.4. Jesus has cut the root of all problems

Before the death and resurrection of Jesus, humankind was afflicted with evil, sickness, death and poverty as a result of the original sin of the first Adam. Jesus cut the root of original sin that was producing evil in our lives and consequently children of God in the time of grace are no longer afflicted by sickness resulting from our sinful past but rather by misunderstanding caused by the root of ignorance. Jesus did not redeem us for sin but from sin. In the Old Testament, humankind was seeking to demonstrate its worth and to conquer sin through good works and obedience of the commandments. However, such an endeavour may be compared to an individual fighting in a battle that has already been lost because of humankind's inherently sinful nature and the fact that all who have sinned have fallen short of the glory of God (Romans 3:23).

Whilst the laws as passed down by Moses effectively gave sin the power to dominate man, grace instead gives man the power to dominate sin. The Bible refers that sin shall not have dominion over you, for you are not under law but under grace (Romans 6:14). Whilst many of God's children understand that we no longer exist under the laws of the Old Testament, they nonetheless continue to live with the mentality practical works are the key to obtaining God's acceptance. Whereas the receipt of God's blessings previously depended upon adherence to the commandments, but under the current time of grace, God's blessings has been bestowed upon humankind as a result of Jesus' obedience to the Father and acceptance of a painful and shameful death of the cross. As such, we are not blessed by our obedience because we are in Christ. Note that Romans 5:19[b] by one man obedience many will be made righteous.

1 Corinthians 15:56 - *'The sting of death is sin, and the strength of sin is the law.' (NKJV)*

Adopting a mentality whereby practical works are considered necessary to obtain God's acceptance effectively gives sin the power to control us. And the devil takes a way to condemn us when we do not perform well. The law empowers sin to control man; however grace empowers man to control sin. Whilst humankind is no longer subject to the laws of the Old Testament, many continue to perceive a need for justification through the performance of good works. It is understandable that to change an individual's mentality and behaviour cannot be done through intimidation and force as this prohibits them from understanding the true reasons why change is required. The life of a child of God is changed when they get to know the person that they are in Christ, which provides the impetus to change their way of living. Knowledge of the good news is crucial for Salvation and for changing our behaviour because the knowledge of the good news reveals our holiness and righteousness in Christ. You are as holy and as righteous as God and you are God's representative on Earth. When one acknowledges this statement, the way of talking, behaving and acting will begin to change because they start to see themselves as different to others.

Romans 2:4 –*'Or do you despise the riches of His goodness, forbearance, and longsuffering, not knowing that the goodness of God leads you to repentance?' (NKJV)*

The following actions may be undertaken in order to assist individuals in changing their lives:

1. Tell them about the unconditional love and goodness of God, which has been manifested through His abundance grace.
2. Help them to understand the type of the person that they are and the type of life that they have in Christ.
3. Tell them that their sins have been forgiven and that they have already been reconciled with God. God holds no ill will towards them for the failures of humankind in the past.

There is a difference between a person who is conscious that they are dressed in clean clothes and one who is conscious that they are dressed in dirty clothes. The one who is dressed in clean clothes will avoid walking in the mud and getting dirty because they are conscious of the person that they are. In contrast, the individual who is already dressing in dirty clothing will have no such reservations as they will possess the mentality that they are already dirty. Many are living unholy life because of lack of knowing their true identity in Christ. The preceding analogy may be compared to the manner in which the Holy Spirit bears witness that we are children of God (Romans 8:16) and convinces us of our state of justice in Christ (John 16:10). The power of the Spirit is a force which affects our way of living because the gospel reveals the righteousness of God to all who believe.

5:

THE LAW OF GOD

5.1. The law has directed to Jesus Christ

The Laws of Moses were passed down from God so that the people of Israel would recognise their sinful state and instruct them towards a more righteous way of life. For contemporary observers, it is important to understand how to reconcile the Old and the New Testament because the two parts of the Bible appear fundamentally different. The Old Testament was the shadow of the things to come and when the reality of those things came, why do we have to continue took at the shadow. That is why such teachings of shadow are not relevant under the dispensation where everything have already been realised through Jesus. We do not reject the Old Testament however we need to study them in the light of the fulfilment of the wonderful work of Jesus. God did not give the laws to humanity in order to save them or to restore the broken relationship with Him but it was given to expose man' sinful nature. Such laws were passed down to humanity on the Sinai Mountain whereby God spoke to Moses and presented him with two tablets of stone and with ceremonial and moral laws.

Romans 3:20 – '*Therefore by the deeds of the law no flesh will be justified in His sight, for by the law is the knowledge of sin.*' (NKJV)

The law was not given to produce Salvation or to forgive the sins of humankind but rather to show people that they are sinners and in need of a saviour. If such laws were not provided, humankind would fail to recognise its sinful state. The law could not transform the inner man because it was directed for the external change and to develop a consciousness of its wrongful behaviours (Romans 7:7-9). The law was not given to make man a better citizen but to direct them to the saviour for their salvation and the transformation of their internal being. As noted by the apostle Paul, before the laws were given, humankind did not know sin and every time it was doing wrong, it had no awareness of such. Through the laws of God as delivered by Moses, humankind came to recognise that whenever they coveted something belonging to others, they were committing sin.

The law was the tutor to bring people to the grace (Jesus Christ) and when Jesus went on the cross to fulfil the law we no longer under this tutor. The important part of the law was to provide a framework to enable us to receive Christ (grace) and to steer us towards Salvation. It is like a supervisor who has a duty to take a child to school' teacher and soon the child is in school the supervisor duty in ended (Galatians 3:24-25). This is why we are not saved by the works of the law but by faith in Jesus Christ who died and resurrected to take away the sins of the entire world.

Under the laws of God, nobody could excuse themselves, nor compare themselves to others because all of humanity had been afflicted by original sin due to the actions of Adam. One may ask - how did all of humanity possess this sinful nature because it was Adam who committed the transgression? The answer is because God had formed one man from dust and all of humanity was descended from Adam – therefore all who are born through a relationship between a father and a mother inherited this nature of original sin of the first Adam (Romans 5:12).

5.2. The Law is incapable to justify

The laws were not provided for individual justification because nobody was capable of obeying all of the commandments that God had given to Israel. One cannot be accepted by God through the justice produced by performing good works (Philippians 3:9), but rather acceptance can only be obtained through the justice that we receive by faith. This is why the citizens of Israel were unable to obtain justice in God because they were seeking to obtain justice by works as opposed to individual faith (Acts 13:38-39).

Animal sacrifices for the purpose of assuaging sin were not pleasing God because there is no harmony between the life of a person and that of an animal. This is why under the Old Covenant sin was not taken away but merely covered up because the transfer of human sins to the life of an animal was a process not desired by God (Hebrew 10:3-6). Animals do not possess human blood and cannot be punished in the place of man. Instead, the high priest was required to go to the holiest place once a year to seek the renewal of the forgiveness of sins committed throughout the year. Animal sacrifices were simply a foreshadowing of what was going to happen on the cross through the death of the true lamb who came to take away sins of all of humanity (John 1:29).

Many religious observers believe that God provided the law of the Old Testament to show humankind what it had to do to become right before God. But that is not so because the law could not make people right on God's sight (Galatians 2:16). The mentality of such law focuses upon "doing" whereas the mentality of grace is about "receiving". Under the dispensation of the law, blessings were received by the obedient whereas those who disobeyed were cursed. Under the dispensation of grace, God's grace and blessings have been made freely available to humankind through the obedience of Jesus and may be drawn down by all those ready to receive such gifts. The mentality of the law pushes people away from God while the mentality of grace draws people near God.

The message of the church is Christocentric – meaning that it focuses upon Jesus and not upon man. The gospel concerns Jesus Christ, not only his name but also what he has done for all of humanity. As such, the focus is not upon what man can do to change his life but rather upon what Jesus has already done to transform the life of humankind. 1Corinthians 3:11 states that 'For no other foundation can anyone lays than that which is laid, which is Jesus Christ. 'This is why Christianity is centred on Jesus and him alone. Jesus said that his church will be built on Christ the son of living God (Matthew 16:18). Unfortunately, many possess a greater understanding of demons and other negative influences compared to their knowledge of Jesus. For many the name of Jesus is used as a slogan at the end of their negative proclamation. As such, many children of God live through the senses of the flesh rather than by faith simply because they possess inadequate knowledge of Jesus Christ. The faith of believer is built on what concern Jesus Christ.

5.3. The influence of Satan

It is important to recognise that Jesus came to set us free; however one must also understand how God made such freedom possible through his influence on Jesus. The key to living a victorious and peaceful life is to understand that God has already set us free by grace (through the death and resurrection of Jesus) and that such freedom is not determined by what we do in our lifetimes. The devil seeks to deceive children of God with the notion that we earn God's peace and blessings through merit and must therefore put our faith and trust in the performance of good works. This is a weapon which the devil seeks to use in order to prevent the children of God from benefitting from the power of the Lord by distorting their focus and influencing their mind. It leads many to place emphasis upon their own endeavours instead of freely receiving from God all that has already been accomplished through grace and goodness (Romans 11:6). We do not deserve the blessings of God, but we are His gracious children.

For instance, many may ask why God has not healed them given that they have prayed and fasted, and are doing their best to receive the blessing of God. Such individuals are focused upon what they are doing for Jesus and not on what Jesus has already done for them. We are healed by grace, blessed by grace and protected by grace and these blessings are manifested through application of our faith. We have all received everything as gift after gift. If one reads the letter of the apostle Paul to the Galatians, it will be noted that Paul did not blame them for committing sins but because of the mixing of the good news of grace with the Law of Moses - which is effectively a law of works. The Jews for example came to tell the Galatians that whilst accepting Jesus is good, it is also necessary to be circumcised and to observe the Mosaic rites. The mixing of grace and law will polluted the power of grace to manifest in people's lives.

Similar beliefs may be observed in the modern world – many believe that you have to live in sanctification before God will accept you or before God to see you. They also believe that no blessings will be received until you have changed your way of living and adopted a sanctified life. This type of mentality places the responsibility on humankind whereas the mentality of grace centralises everything on Jesus. We have already mentioned that our good doing changes us towards God because He has already anticipated everything before even us to know Him. The love, goodness and blessings of God are not conditional. In the time of grace in which we are living, when you place trust in good works alongside trust in grace, it prevents complete manifestation of the powers of God. Conversely, when you place complete trust in grace, you will experience the full glory of God in your life.

5.4. The Law was fulfilled

There are certain subjects in the Bible that cannot be fully understood if we do not understand the concepts of dispensations and Covenants. In the Bible, there are approximately eight dispensations which may be in fact reduced to four and these relate to the relationship between humanity and God depending upon the time when such individuals were living. For example, in the Edenic dispensation (known the dispensation of innocence), the relationship between God and humankind was direct and stable because humankind existed one hundred percent in the nature of God. After this period was ended by the original sin, God was seeking to restore the relationship back to its original position. Moving forward to the time of Abraham, who was living under the dispensation of conscious, the relationship between God and humanity had not yet been conditioned because God had yet to decree the laws which would provide a behavioural framework for human life. Indeed, the Bible teaches us that Abraham was not justified by good works but by faith. Abraham had in fact committed mistakes which would have been condemned by the future laws of Moses including taking his sister as a wife but it is known that Abraham was living before the Law of Moses. The next period was characterised as the 'dispensation of law 'whereby Moses conveyed God's laws to humankind and emphasis was placed upon individual merit and obedience. If one were to ask Moses what a sin was, he would likely respond that a sin is a transgression of the law. Finally, following the death and resurrection of Jesus Christ, the dispensation of law ended and was replaced by the 'dispensation of grace'.

As set out above, each dispensation represented a different stage in the relationship between God and humanity and God was dealing to people according to the dispensation they were living. God never changed however life on Earth was changing. Each dispensation was based upon a specific covenant and mentality established by God and is described in further detail below:

The dispensation of innocence: This began from the time that God formed man until the day that man ate from the tree of knowledge of good and bad. At this time, man knew neither good nor bad, suffering nor death. He had no negative mentality within him and his nature was perfect as God.

Example of a person who was under this dispensation: Adam.

The dispensation of conscious: This period began with the fall of man and lasted until the time when Moses received the Ten Commandments on Mount Sinai. People under this regime were living according to their own devices and free will because God had not yet bequeathed the laws to humankind.

Example of a person was living under this dispensation: Abraham.

The dispensation of law: This period began with the receipt of the Ten Commandments on Mount Sinai and lasted until the death of Jesus on the cross.

Example of a person who was living under this dispensation: Moses.

The dispensation of grace: This period began on the cross when Jesus absorbed the sin of the world when he cried out that it is finish and will end when the church is taken away.

Example of a person who is living under this dispensation: All of us.

The original sin of Adam corrupted the inherent nature of mankind. We inherit this sinful nature through birth. As such, a baby who is born may not know how to speak or perform evil actions but will nonetheless be categorised as a sinner (Psalms 51:5). In contrast, we receive the nature and justice of God through re-births which occurs on the day that we believe and accept Jesus into our lives.

The original sin Adam provided the root that enabled the devil to dominate us and resulted in sickness and evil actions. Jesus cut this root by becoming the sinful nature of humankind through his death on the cross. Such sin nature died in and with the body of Jesus and on the third day Jesus was resurrected as a new creature. Knowing that Jesus was the first man to be born again that why the Bible states that he is the first born among many. Anyone who believes and receives Jesus Christ participates in the reality of the death and the resurrection of Jesus, this is the reason the Bible declares that if anyone is in Christ, he is a new creation. A child of God is not anymore a sinner because they do not have the sin nature anymore, as God is, so are the children of God in this world (1 John 4:17). However, a sinner is the one who still have the sin nature of the first Adam. The death of Jesus has made possible a transformation in the relationship of between humankind and God. For those who believe in the fulfilled work of Jesus, such sin of nature no longer exists for them. Any individual who has accepted and received Jesus as his/her personal Lord and saviour have been completely transformed through a spiritual rebirth.

Romans 5:12 –'*Therefore, just as through one man sin entered the world, and death through sin, and thus death spread to all men…' (NKJV)*

As set out in the extract from Romans above, through the actions of Adam, everybody became a sinner; it is not individual actions which make a person a sinner but rather their inherent nature which has been inherited from Adam. Yet, if we believe that we became sinners through the actions of one man then we must also believe that we are no longer sinners because we have been born again in the nature of Christ. Jesus restored the broken relationship and gave us the justice of God through thc sacrifice he made for us.

6:

SALVATION IS A DONE DEAL

6.1. Once for All

The work of Jesus Christ was undertaken for the benefit of the entire world however humankind has the reciprocal responsibility to respond to what Jesus has done. Jesus went to the cross once and he will not go back to do it again. A useful analogy is a supply agreement which a household may possess with an energy company - it is not the company's responsibility to attend the premises each time you require electricity but instead it is up to you to press the switch in order to draw current. Every will and plan of God was fully done one and for all the time. The light of the book of Hebrew compares the work of the priests during the time of the Old Covenant and the work of Jesus who is effectively our High priest. Whereas sacrifices were made routinely during the time of the Old Testament, Jesus' sacrifice on the cross was made once, for all of God's creation and will last until the end of time (Hebrew 9:26-28).

The sacrifice on the cross is a complete work which has been achieved for all of humankind and will benefit all generations without distinction until the end of time. Under the Old Covenant, the high priest was required to enter the most holy site once a year to make sacrifices and seek the forgiveness of sins. Such activities were a foreshadowing of the sacrifice to be undertaken by Jesus which was performed only once because according the language of God, the dispensation of grace has only one year (Luke 4:19).When Jesus saw that God the Father was satisfied with his work to accept mankind into His presence on the basis of a renewed relationship, John 19:30 notes that he cried out "It is finished." The veil of the temple which had previously separated the holy place and the most holy site was torn in two from the top to bottom and the most holy place which was only previously accessible to the high priest had become available to all priests. This means that communion with God had become possible for all priests who entered the holy place.

God has made all of His children priests (Revelation 5:10) - that is why the presence of God dwells in us and we dwell in the presence of God (1John 3:24). Jesus went to the cross and paid the price of death once, he has shared his blood once, he has delivered us once, he has forgiven and sanctified us once and he has justified us once. Consequently it is imperative that we understand that although Jesus' sacrifice was made once for all two thousand years ago, the benefits of such a sacrifice and manifestation of God's power continue until the present time.

It is important to know that all the will and plan of God was already fulfilled and given to us, we are not looking for them but must instead discover them through knowledge and obtain a detailed awareness which will enable us to experience the life of God. Jesus' victory over the devil is permanent and we must recognise this in our minds as well as is in our spirits - this is why the Bible states that we are more than conquerors (Romans 8:37). Our faith functions on what Jesus has already accomplished and not on visible manifestations. Whilst those living in the time of the earthly ministry of Jesus based their faith on his physical presence, but our faith is based upon all that has been written and through our beliefs we have a life in Jesus Christ.

When Jesus was physically beaten, wounded and chastised as part of his quest to fulfil the will of God, he was being punished and judged in our place and by his stripes we were healed. It is important for humankind to activate its faith because God will never again repeat the work of sacrificing His son and His healing, peace and grace is already within us. When the Holy Spirit descended upon us, it carried all of God's blessings this is why the apostle Peter tells us that through divine power (Who is the Holy Spirit) we have received everything that pertains to life (2 Peter 1:3).

Many children of God do not accept this truth because they are seeking physical and emotional evidence in order to justify their beliefs. However, the faith which God has given us is multidimensional and functions in two realms - it takes what is spiritual and manifests such phenomena physically. God could not simply forgive the sins of humanity but was required to make a sacrifice of blood and this price was not paid to the devil but rather to enable God to accept us back into His house. Whilst Jesus had a physical body in human form, he was not a sinner because his body was not the product of man and woman. This is why Jesus knew no sin but was able to deliver those who had the bodies of sin because sin was the cause of man's separation from God.

6.2. The person that I am in Christ

God is spirit and He has created us in spiritual form -to be in contact with Him and with the Eternity – and He has formed us in physical form in order to reign in the tangible world. We know that humankind is spirit, has a soul and lives in the physical body. A child of God is completely unique and has been recreated as a new creature in the image of God as our old man was dead and buried with Jesus. We are products of the resurrection because children of God were not only saved from their old nature but were completely transformed (2 Corinthians 3:18). Our spirit has been transformed from its original state to the form in which it will exist for eternity. God dwells in the spirit of all those who have been saved because in the act of being born again our spirit was recreated in God's image and to function like Christ. In our spirit, we are holy and righteous like Christ and all of the power which was in Jesus is also in every child of God. Just as we have a mirror that helps us to observe our physical appearance, we also have a mirror that enables us to look at our spirit and this is the good news of the abundance of grace of

Jesus. Ultimately, the life of a child of God is from the inside to the outside because the person that exists on the inside has the power to influence the outside.

1 John 2:20–'*But you have an anointing from the Holy one, and you know all things.' (NKJV)*

When we study a passage such as the above, it is important to recognise that this verse concerns our spirit because in our spirit we have the same anointing that was in Jesus and we possess knowledge of God. This type of verse cannot be considered in physical and emotional sides but in our spirit born again. In our soul part as children of God we continue to learn each day and consequently many will have difficulty comprehending the extract above and may not believe it because they think man is only a physical part that they see. That is why such teachings have been written down for us to know and by knowing them we in turn believe them. The spirit of a child of God is complete with the fullness of everything (Colossians 2:10) - when we understand and are conscious of these privileges, faith will intervene to make this a reality in both the physical and mental realm. God has given us the eyes of faith which enable us to see ourselves in the spirit through the good news. All the blessings of God are in us, the spirit of a child of God lacks nothing because it has been completely blessed. When we were born again, our spirit was sealed with the Holy Spirit and therefore our spirit cannot be touched by the evil and no one can steal what God has already placed within us.

The devil operates by preventing children of God from discovering themselves through the light of the gospel. This is important because the good news is not the revelation of the condemnation of human being but it is the revelation of the justice of God for man. However, not knowing who you are and what you have been given by God does not preclude the existence of blessings within you; as such blessings are ever present despite individual ignorance. We believe what we know, what we know forms our thoughts and this in turn impacts upon our way of living.

Ephesians 1:13 – *'In Him you also trusted, after you heard the word of truth, the gospel of your Salvation; in whom also, having believed, you were sealed with the Holy Spirit of promise…'* (NKJV)

The Good News Translation of the above passage uses the phrase 'put his stamp' whereas the New King James Version has used the term 'sealed'. The verb 'sealed 'as contained in this verse has two meanings. Firstly, this word refers to the security of all goods (blessings) that we have received through Salvation – which means that nobody has the power to destroy or to steal them because everything that God has given us is in that sealed spirit. Secondly, this word sealed also implies belonging; every product has a seal which indicates who made and/or owns it. Every Christian is a private property of God and is therefore untouchable because they are sealed. This concept may be compared to an empty bottle which has been filled with liquid and sealed with a lid, thereby rendering this liquid untouchable and unaffected by outside influences. The Bible teaches us that we are in God's hands and nobody is able to snatch us from his loving grip. This forms the security of our lives and all that we have received in Christ. This concept of protection may be illustrated when we put insects in a clear bottle well sealed and we expose it in the middle of chickens, they will not be able to eat these insects because of the safety and the protection that they have in the bottle. The life of a child of God with all the blessings is well secured and protected in the Holy Spirit.

As Christ is, so we are all the children of God. One must not look themselves in the flesh but rather in the spirit. We do not possess the nature of God but instead we are the nature of God because God created humankind in His own nature and transformed us through the Holy Spirit on the day that we believed and received Jesus into our lives. Many children of God are ignorant to this truth and are living outside of their true nature because their eyes are limited to only seeing the physical and emotional parts of their being.

Every child of God is powerful on Earth because all of the power of God dwells in his/her spirit. When God told us to cast out demons and to heal the sick He knew that we possessed sufficient authority because God would not send us to do something that we are incapable of doing. He is a faithful Father.

6.3. The reconciliation of God and Humanity

The Bible teaches us that we have sinned and fallen short of the glorious presence of God (Romans 3:23). Humanity has been separated from God and the relationship broken as a result of original sin. Salvation provided the means for God to deliver us from the dangers caused by original sin. God himself came to solve the problem and He has facilitated reconciliation through the death and resurrection of His son Jesus Christ. Humankind was unable to return to its source because of the barrier created by sin that Jesus came to break.

2 Corinthians 5:19 –'*…God was in Christ reconciling the world to Himself…'* (NKJV)

Through Salvation, God came to redeem His own nature because God was in Christ to forgive and to reconcile the world to Himself. The verb 'reconcile' means 'to make again one 'and is often used in the context of financial settings – for example when somebody seeks to reconcile discrepancies in personal or business accounts. Similarly, the prefix're' is used to signify something that has previously been done and is being done for the second time.

God wanted to restore his relationship with humankind to the same position which had existed in the Garden of Eden. Notice that it was God who came to man for reconciliation, yet it was man who had disobeyed God. It was not man who loved God first, but it was God who loved man. This is proof of the unconditional love of God for his creation. Being one with God is purely the will and choice of God because he acts according to the nature of His love (1 John 4:8). Reconciliation is not a future ambition, but it has already been achieved through the death and resurrection of Jesus because humankind is already with God and has been recreated His nature. This is why everybody who became a child of God is one with God and it is important to know that we assume this position through faith in all that Jesus has accomplished for us.

Reconciliation brought us back to God, we dwell in God and He dwells in our spirit and all the full presence of God is in the believer and this presence is a place where we were born and we live. We do not go to God and we do not enter His presence because we are already there, it is our dwelling place. Another reason why we do not go to God because He is always with us we are always with Him because we were born in His presence. Our unity with God is achieved through the spirit because God no longer has a physical body on Earth. We are truly one spirit with God (1Corinthians 6:17), our spirit is divine and filled with all of the gifts that have been provided by God. We must be confident in the person that we are in spirit as the key to living a victorious life on Earth is to live in harmony with the person that we are in spirit. When I am working in reality it is the Holy Spirit who is working and the physical body of the believer is the temple of God. Be conscious of the presence of God and it is with the believer everywhere a believer goes.

6.4. Transformed in the image of Christ

On the day of Salvation, humankind was totally transformed in spirit by the Holy Spirit according to the image of God the creator. The true identity of a child of God is determined according to the inner person who is recreated in God image. This transformation will not happen when the believer will be in Eternity but it is now and is the reason that our faith is based upon the power of God because we believe the good news that is being proclaimed. When the Bible says that we received the righteousness of God, we don't physically observe such a gift however our faith sees and believes this truth. Many children of God have difficulty understanding who they are in Christ because they are looking for physical manifestations as opposed to seeing it in the reality of their spirit. God is Spirit and He does everything first in spirit, including communication with humankind. As His children, it is our duty to learn to see ourselves in the reality of the spirit and this is possible by faith in the light of the gospel. Jesus reminded the believer to know that they are gods (John 10:34) and the life that they are living is not natural but supernatural.

2 Corinthians 5:17 - *Therefore, if anyone is in Christ, he is a new creation; old things have passed away; behold, all things have become new.' (NKJV)*

All who have accepted and believed that Jesus Christ is his/her saviour is a new character which never existed before. This new creature was created in Christ; it has not been repaired or modified but instead has been created again in the nature of Christ. Those who are born again have been justified to be righteous in the state of a new person who has never sinned. Such individuals are superior to the devil and are untouchable because they are powerful like Christ himself. We are born from glory and victory with all God's blessings. The grace of God has privileged us to take part of the inheritance of the saints, this is the reason thanksgiving is our everyday prayer. We are born again in the righteousness of God and we pay nothing to deserve it (Romans 5:17) but someone paid for it with the price of his life. We have to understand that the gift of righteousness makes us reign in life through Christ. Being righteousness of God is free gifts that every believer has received and when we believe this revelation it empower the life to work in victory. Reigning in life means that we have dominion over all the evil influences and we ruling in life. This is the reason we have the authority over the devil and demons because we are kings in the Kingdom of God. Jesus accepted his sacrifice on the cross in order to share his blood and unlock the gifts which have been bestowed upon humanity.

The first sentence of 2 Corinthians 5:18 states 'Now all are things of God…' and whilst we may not see any changes in our physical reality, we should recognise that we are a product of grace through the work of God. Becoming a new person in Christ does not occur because of good works - if this was the case then all who perform good works or charitable deeds would be born again. Being born again takes place when an individual becomes one in Christ by believing the word of God which in turn enables the Holy Spirit to enter and to transform the inner man (1 Peter 1:23). This new person assumes the complete nature of God in the same manner that babies assume their parent's nature through DNA. In our born again spirit we possess God's DNA because we are born from Him. Anyone who is born again is holy, pure, without fault and blameless like God because God sees the believer in their born again spirit sitting with Christ in the heavenly places. This is also made them superior and more powerful than the devil, if the believer would like to write a letter to the devil, it must to be under the feet.

1 Corinthians 15:42-49 –*'So will it be with the resurrection of the dead. The body that is sown is perishable; it is raised in imperishable…' (NIV)*

When Jesus was buried, we were with him and when he was resurrected, we were also with him. The passage above from Corinthians identifies two bodies that carry two different natures - there is natural body and the spiritual body. The natural body is in the nature of Adam (the first man formed from dust) - this body became the body of sin when Adam ate the fruit of the tree of knowledge of good and bad. The spiritual body is in the nature of the last Adam (Jesus Christ), knowing that Jesus is the last

Adam because there will not be another saviour as he is the only saviour. 1 Corinthians 15:48 states 'As was the earthly man, so are those who are of the earth' – highlighting the linkage between humankind and first Adam who was formed from dust. This also implies that all those who have not yet been saved are sinners because of the original sin of the first Adam. In stating '…as is the heavenly man, so also are those who are of heaven', the apostle Paul is noting that those who have been saved are in the same nature as Christ. One must not regard themselves as a sinner because you are in the nature of Christ and not in the nature of a sinner. Whenever you see yourself as a sinner you are exposing yourself to manipulation by the devil and exposing yourself to the negative influences, and will consequently live and behave like a sinner. If one commits a mistake in life it will not change their nature. Similarly, if an individual performs good works but does not believe and accept God's sacrifice, they cannot change their nature and become holy.

6.5. The attainment of Salvation

Many people struggle to understand the concept of Salvation and a number of false ideas have been circulated by observers in terms of how Salvation is obtained. Salvation is simple to receive but some people make it hard by putting many emphases in what to do.

In Acts 16:31, the apostle Paul said to the keeper of the prison, "Believe in the Lord Jesus Christ, and you will be saved, you and your household." Paul did not ask the keeper to do anything else except to believe, because Salvation is not the work of man but rather that of God Himself. We believe that Jesus died for our sins and was resurrected in order to save us. Salvation is not received by the application of the verb 'to do' but rather by the verb 'to believe'. We do not receive Jesus physically but through the words that is proclaimed in the good news of grace. And these words are so powerful to transform the inner man.

Romans 10:9-10 – '*...that if you confess with your mouth the Lord Jesus and believe in your heart that God has raised Him from the dead, you will be saved...' (NKJV)*

When we believe in something, we accept it as truth and when we confess it, it means we agree that it is so for our lives. When one believes in their heart that Jesus died and was resurrected for them, they align themselves with the same thoughts of God and through confession it becomes a reality. Jesus went to the cross in order to suffer and to share his blood in order to take away sins of all. Through the fulfilment of his mission, he has established the relationship between God and humanity, and we participate in this New Covenant when we put our faith in Jesus and in all that he has accomplished. Salvation is available to everybody – Jesus 'sacrifice was made once and for all and will not be repeated because it remains relevant for all generations until he returns to Earth. The responsibility to receive this Salvation is on humans. Those who are not yet saved can receive Salvation simply by receiving and believing Jesus Christ as the saviour of their lives. God has played His part of sacrificing His son Jesus for the whole world and in the other side man has a part to play to receive salvation.

We become children of God in the moment of Salvation because the Holy Spirit enter in the believer spirit to make the death and the resurrection a reality in the person' life and the Holy Spirit confirm the salvation as the Bible states that the Spirit bears witness with man's spirit that we are children of God (Romans 8:16). God is our Father and we have become heirs of God and joint heirs with Christ by possessing all that belong to God (Romans 8:17).

We become children of God by fulfilling two acts on the day of Salvation - receiving and believing Jesus Christ through the word (John 1:12). Whilst Jesus died for all of humanity, not everybody is classed as a child of God because many have not received and believed in the son of God. A familial relationship exists between God and those who are saved - a relationship between the Father and a child.

Yet this is not the same as a father-child relationship in the human form because spirits have no gender. The word father in Hebrew is 'Abba', meaning 'source', 'provider' and 'leader'. The same God the Father who is in the Eternity is in us, hence why when we pray to the Father, our prayers do not go up to heaven but are instead listened inside us because the Father is in our spirit. The same God the Father who is in heavens is also in every believer.

If you believe in your heart that the Lord Jesus died and was resurrected for you, a prayer has been set out below through which you can express gratitude and glory to God. Repeat this prayer after me:

Lord Jesus, I believe that you died for my sins. You were condemned, judged and punished in my place. I believe that God has raised you from the dead and I receive you as my personal saviour and Lord, Amen.

In reciting this prayer on a regular basis with sincerity of the heart, you are saved; one can transform their being and become a child in God's family. All of your sins are taken away and all that Jesus has accomplished on the cross and through his resurrection are now a reality in you. God is your Father - you have become a citizen of the Kingdom of God and you also now have the rights and privileges associated with being one of His children. Congratulation! Welcome in God's family.

A declaration of faith has also been set out below which, upon profession, will help to manifest what are inside of you:

I (name) am a beloved child of God, I am an heir of God, I have divine health, I refuse to be sick and I proclaim healing in my body. I am completely free in

every area of my life; there are no demonic influences in my life because I am more than a conqueror. I am victorious, I refuse poverty and I am a gracious child, in the name of Jesus, Amen.

CONCLUSION

This book has sought to explain the fundamental tenets of Christian life and has examined in detail key extracts of the word of God which will enable us to live a more stable life under God's blessing on earth. Being a child of God is a privileged position because the Bible tells us that those who are born of God live triumphantly in the world. It also means that one is no longer subject to the devil's deceptive influence and can instead live in the Kingdom of God and reign as kings.

God, by His love, anticipated the needs of humanity before humanity even came into existence and this proves the depth of God's unconditional love for the entire world. We do not deserve the love of God, but His grace has opened the door for us to benefit from such love. Consequently, in our day to day lives, we must not rely on our own physical efforts and good works but rather trust in the unmerited favour of God instead. We were once disqualified from God's love as a result of the original sin however Jesus has restored the relationship between God and humankind, and we have now been qualified through God's grace. Salvation is not a human initiative but is instead a privilege that we have received by God's unconditional love. Notwithstanding the above, many children of God remain ignorant of the sacrifices made on their behalf and need to shift their mental focus away from physical performances and towards a more intimate understanding of the gifts of God. Only the truth that you know will set you free because what you do not know will not work for you. Your freedom is not based upon continually battling demons because Jesus has already set you but through knowing who you are and what you possess in Christ. Lack of knowing what the Lord Jesus has done is one of the ways many are not fully experiencing the life of God that they have. The devil and all demons were disarmed on the cross and were thereby nullified and stripped of their powers. The devil is unable to touch those who belong to God because their lives are hidden in God and they are fully protected by God and they are in total security - nothing will harm you. Unfortunately, many spend too much time talking and thinking about demons and the devil – this in turn becomes a way to glorify the devil and it draws an individual's full attention onto him. Rather, what we need to do is to place more emphasis upon exalting the name of Jesus and all that he has done. This approach will diminish the force of all problems because the name of Jesus has been highly exalted above all names and in his name all knees must bow.

We are now living in the dispensation of grace, in a time whereby Jesus has fulfilled everything and left nothing for us to fulfil. Each of us has the mission to proclaim the work that the Lord Jesus Christ has done for humanity through the good news that God has already reconciled with all humanity. He paid the price that we were incapable of paying for our freedom and we need to believe in the good news that we are free indeed. Let us rejoice that our freedom has been offered by the grace of Jesus. We are the beloved children of God.

CONTACT INFORMATION

If you would like any help or support throughout your journey with Christ, please do not hesitate to contact Destined to Reign Church at the address below:

Destined to Reign Church
75-81 King Street
Dudley
West Midlands
DY2 8QB
United Kingdom

Website: www.destoreignchurch.org

Email: destoreign@yahoo.com

Tel.: +44 (0)1384 230707

Available worldwide from Amazon

www.mtp.agency

@mtp_agency

www.facebook.com/mtp.agency

Michael Terence
Publishing

Printed in Great Britain
by Amazon

55052969R00064